Original title:
Orange Blossom Breeze

Copyright © 2025 Creative Arts Management OÜ
All rights reserved.

Author: Alexander Thornton
ISBN HARDBACK: 978-1-80586-464-6
ISBN PAPERBACK: 978-1-80586-936-8

Sunshine in a Garden's Embrace

In the garden, sunlight dances,
Petals laughing, taking chances.
Bees are buzzing, humming tunes,
While flowers sway like silly goons.

Butterflies wear flashy clothes,
Twisting, turning, striking poses.
A gopher peeks with curious eyes,
And blinks at blooms in bright disguise.

Light Glistening on Petal Faces

Raindrops sparkle on soft curls,
Nature's chuckle, twirls and swirls.
Each petal wears a shiny hat,
As a squirrel waves—look at that!

Sunbeams giggle through the leaves,
While busy ants plot their heaves.
They march in lines, their tiny trek,
Chasing shadows with great quirk.

Playful Fragrance on the Wind

A scent of mischief fills the air,
Playful whispers everywhere.
Twirling scents, a jolly spree,
Makes the daisies dance with glee.

The fragrant breeze knows all the tricks,
It tickles noses, plays like six.
A cheeky rose winks at the sun,
Inviting everyone to run!

Uplifted by Flowery Hues

In hues so bright, they cheer us on,
Each bloom grinning at the dawn.
Petunia's giggle, lily's grin,
Make even grumpy faces spin.

Colors clash in a happy fight,
Silly blossoms, pure delight.
A daffodil trips over its shoes,
While nature sings its joyful blues.

The Flicker of Sunshine Among Petals

In gardens where giggles collide,
Bees dance a waltz, with pride.
Petals are hats for the bumblebees,
While butterflies play hide and tease.

Sunshine flickers, a playful sprite,
Tickling flowers with pure delight.
Laughter bursts from the blooms on high,
As daisies drop jokes and daffodils sigh.

Where Sweetness Meets the Sky

Clouds fluff up like cotton candy,
While giggling winds feel quite dandy.
Lemonades mix with the bright blue air,
Giving butterflies jokes to share.

The sun's a clown in a golden suit,
Juggling rays with an orange fruit.
Sipping nectar from cups made of dew,
While petals snicker, 'Oh, who knew?'

Soft Footfalls on Scented Trails

A squirrel with flair prances around,
Chasing his shadow, it leaps off the ground.
With soft footfalls, a mischief galore,
He trips on a flower, then rolls on the floor.

Scented trails beckon with giggle-filled dreams,
Where nature's aroma tickles with beams.
Running amok, oh what a sight,
As rabbits join in, hopping with light.

The Lure of Citrusy Expanse

A twist of zest whirls in the air,
Where laughter flutters without a care.
Lemons chuckle, tangy and bright,
As limes wink back in sheer delight.

In the stretch where the sun meets the cheek,
Jokes sprout in rows, all joyous and cheek.
Plants gossip about fruity quips,
As nature enjoys its hilarious trips.

Radiant Petals on the Wind

The flowers giggle as they sway,
Their fragrance tickles, come what may.
Bees wear sunglasses, oh so cool,
Chatting with petals, what a fun rule!

A butterfly slides on a slip and slide,
Laughter erupts, it's a joyous ride.
A ladybug joins with a tiny dance,
In this floral circus, all take a chance!

Echoes of Zestful Whispers

Petal whispers tickle our ears,
As the sunshine spills joyful cheers.
A bumblebee buzzes a silly tune,
Dancing with daisies under the moon.

A wind gust knocks the ants in a row,
They tumble and giggle, what a show!
With snickers and chuckles from all around,
This is the best kind of sound!

Sunlit Blooms and Gentle Winds

Sunshine drapes on blooms with flair,
As petals plot a mischievous dare.
They wiggle and jiggle, no time to pause,
Creating a ruckus, just because!

Breezes blow in, like playful friends,
Spreading the charm that never ends.
A squirrel joins in, his tail in a knot,
Forgetting his acorns, a silly plot!

The Dance of Scented Petals

In the garden's heart, a party blooms,
The flowers waltz, shedding their glooms.
A dancer slips, and petals take flight,
This comical scene is pure delight!

The breeze suggests we all unite,
Clumsy steps make the laughter ignite.
Let's twirl and chuckle, in this fragrant spree,
Where petals bounce high, and ants groove free!

Radiant Beauty on Garden Trails

In the garden, where laughter sways,
Flowers giggle in comical displays.
Bees in tuxedos, buzzing with flair,
Dance off the petals, without a care.

A squirrel wearing shades, oh what a sight,
Chasing the sun, full of delight.
The daisies burst out with silly pranks,
While roses blush red, giving their thanks.

Luminescent Hues at Daybreak

Sunrise splashes colors, bright and bold,
Daffodils whisper gossip that's told.
A hummingbird hovers, giggling with glee,
Stealing sweet nectar, what a carefree spree!

The early worms yawn as the sun lifts high,
Wiggling and jiggling beneath a blue sky.
Frogs croak their verses in a comical tune,
While butterflies waltz to the morning's saloon.

Serene Flip of Petal and Leaf

Petals twirl around as they take a spin,
Leaves clap their hands, let the fun begin.
A ladybug laughs, wearing polka-dot glee,
As dandelions puff like balloons on a spree.

The ivy starts creeping but trips on a vine,
While grasshoppers joke, as they sip on sweet wine.
The roses pose, striking a funny old pout,
While vines tease the weeds, wiggling about.

A Kiss of Citrus on the Breeze

The wind carries giggles, sweet as a prank,
Lemons chuckle softly in their zesty tank.
Limes toss up jokes that zing through the air,
While tangerines tumble down without a care.

In this fruity fiesta, everyone shines,
Mandarins dance in bright, citrusy lines.
Even the zest seems to tickle and tease,
As laughter bounces in the warm, sunny breeze.

Lullabies from Blooming Canopies

Under twinkling stars, we dance and sway,
Laughter drips like honey, lighting up the way.
A squirrel in a hat chases shadows so bold,
Reminding us all that life never gets old.

With petals like pillows, they float in the breeze,
Birds strut in tuxedos, inviting us to tease.
As cicadas sing tunes that tickle our ears,
We giggle and bounce, forgetting our fears.

Ambrosial Currents at Twilight

A toast to the nectar served under the sky,
Where fireflies flutter, each flair a sly cry.
The moon whispers secrets, all wrapped up in glee,
As we nibble on cookies beneath the tall tree.

With giggles like bubbles that pop in midair,
Our jokes fly like kites, unaware of the snare.
The breeze steals our hats, playful and spry,
Two llamas steal popcorn, oh my, oh my!

The Essence of Fruitful Days

In gardens where laughter spills over the vine,
A jester in overalls insists he can rhyme.
His shoes squeak like violins, much to our cheer,
As tomatoes play catch with the cucumbers near.

Berries burst like laughter, ripe for the picking,
While bees do the tango, oh how they are kicking!
With every sweet bite, we whirl and we twirl,
In this carnival world, it's our fruity unfurl.

Vibrant Caress of the Afternoon

A picnic of giggles on a blanket so wide,
Where sandwiches wear hats and form quite the pride.
The lemonade's fizzy, a bubbly delight,
As ants in top hats march, stealing our sight.

Bananas throw parties, quite silly they are,
Inviting the sun and each twinkling star.
With a sprinkle of joy, we all share a tune,
In the warmth of the afternoon, magic will bloom.

The Caress of Petal-Laden Breezes

In the garden, petals dance,
Waving to the bees, they prance.
Stumbling on their own sweet scent,
A cotton candy world is spent.

Fluffy clouds compete for space,
While butterflies wear a silly face.
They gossip with a rustling laugh,
As ants take the tiniest path.

A squirrel thinks he's quite the star,
Zooming past on a nutty car.
The breeze carries tales of joy,
To each flower, every toy.

With each gust, the sunbeams tease,
Caressing the branches with the breeze.
All around, the colors tease,
Nature's mischief never flees.

Hues Softened by the Sun

Today the sky wore lovely hues,
All dressed up in bright, sunny shoes.
A bumblebee lost his way,
Buzzing on for a fun-filled day.

The daisies giggled in a row,
Whispering secrets only they know.
The sun played peek-a-boo so sly,
While clouds wore hats that drifted by.

A dog tried fetching joy, oh dear,
But tripped and rolled, it's quite unclear.
He swirled like paint across the grass,
Painting laughter as moments pass.

When the evening sun takes flight,
Colors swirl in a playful light.
Every petal, a little tease,
Softened hues bring cheerful knees.

Blossoms Drifting on Gentle Currents

Blossoms drift upon the stream,
Like fluffy pillows in a dream.
They giggle as they spin in glee,
While waving 'hi' to every bee.

A fish peeks up, surprised and bold,
Catching petals, a sight to behold.
It chuckles as it takes a dive,
Who knew such madness could survive?

Breezes carry whispers sweet,
That tickle toes and dance on feet.
Nature's prankster plays its role,
As every blossom claims its soul.

They float along, a carefree band,
Creating joy at nature's hand.
With petals bobbing by the shore,
Who knew plants could laugh so much more?

Celestial Notes of Fragrant Life

Under the sky's melodious notes,
Flowers jam with buzzing goats.
A rabbit hops in rhythm fine,
Making tunes with a twist of vine.

The wind strums leaves, a leafy choir,
With laughter that never seems to tire.
Sunlight dapples all around,
As giggles swirl without a sound.

Upside down, a mushroom sings,
Life's silly dance is full of swings.
The daisies join in, can't resist,
Adding to the prankster's twist.

With every fragrance, joy takes flight,
A symphony of pure delight.
Celestial notes fill up the air,
Life's fragrance is beyond compare.

Gentle Sways of a Sunlit Afternoon

The trees are dancing, what a sight,
Leaves flapping wildly, oh what a fright!
Squirrels giggle in their playful chase,
While bees in hats pick up the pace.

A cat in shades lounges on a fence,
Winking at birds that seem quite dense.
A dog rolls by, a comical show,
Chasing its tail like it's in slow-mo.

The sun leans down with a friendly grin,
As laughter rings out like a joyful din.
A tiny ant with a hefty crumb,
Struggles ahead with a tiny hum.

With giggles mixed in the light warm breeze,
All worries float, like leaves from trees.
In this sunny swirl, we all can play,
Sipping lemonade till the end of day.

Petal Play in the Luminous Glow

Petals twirl in the soft sunlight,
Like ballerinas in a playful flight.
Butterflies giggle with elegant flair,
Their sparkly wings glide through the air.

A dandelion sneezes, poof! It's gone,
Kids chase the fluff till the sun's withdrawn.
They tumble and roll, all laughter and cheer,
Swirling and spinning, nothing to fear.

A rabbit hops in a wild disguise,
Wearing a bowtie, oh what a surprise!
Each hop a joke, each leap a jest,
In this garden stage, they're all the best.

As evening falls with a twinkling hue,
The petals and creatures bid adieu.
But in their hearts, the fun will stay,
Till laughter blooms back another day.

Breezes Carrying Aromatic Tales

A waft of sweetness drifts through the park,
With scents of cookies that hit like a spark.
A candle nearby tips over with ease,
Sending a whiff of it wafting on breeze.

A skunk strolls by, tail held high,
Mistaken for perfume—oh my, oh my!
The birds all scoff, they cover their beaks,
As giggles burst out in animated squeaks.

The flowers chime in, a fragrant debate,
Which one's the best? Is it mint? Or is it date?
They bump into bees who buzz with delight,
Having a blast in their pollens' flight.

As the day fades, and shadows grow chill,
Notes of laughter linger, a sweet sound still.
Each breeze carries stories, each rustle a tease,
Turning our frowns into joy with such ease.

Sunrise Serenade of Color

The dawn breaks brightly, a canvas so bold,
Cats stretch and yawn, with stories untold.
A rooster sings out, but off-key, of course,
The beasts roll their eyes, "What a funny force!"

The flowers wake with a colorful cheer,
Flashing their petals, "Come dance over here!"
A robin trips over a dewdrop surprise,
As the sun plays peekaboo, brightening the skies.

A raccoon tops off his breakfast with flair,
As squirrels gather, having fun with their hair.
With mischief in shadows, they plot a quick snack,
Debating which berry they'll grab from the stack.

So raise a glass to this vibrant awakening,
With giggles and grins, the day is unshaking.
In every corner, color glows bright,
Let's dance with delight in the morning light!

Citrus Whispers in the Wind

In the garden, a cat did prance,
She chased a bug in a silly dance.
A citrus tree watched with a grin,
While lemons giggled, oh, where to begin?

The breeze caught a joke from the vine,
As oranges chuckled, feeling divine.
Lime and grapefruit joined in the jest,
Together they whispered, 'We're simply the best!'

Fragrant Dreams of Sunlit Gardens

A squirrel in bloom with a fruity hat,
Mistook a lemon for a cozy mat.
He settled down for an afternoon nap,
Unaware he'd cause quite the mishap!

The flowers laughed, their petals shook,
As bees paused to take a better look.
'Just a lemon,' they buzzed with ease,
Who knew a rodent could bring us such tease?

Fluttering Petals of Early Spring

A parrot named Lou loved to proclaim,
He fancied himself quite the citrus name!
With squawks of zest and a flair for fun,
He'd steal the show, outshining the sun!

Honing his act with goofy tricks,
He'd juggle oranges, what a mix!
The garden fell silent, then burst into cheers,
As the fruits danced along, laughing in years!

Sweet Nectar of Dusk's Embrace

As twilight fell, the fruits held a ball,
With lemons in tuxes, making a call.
Grapefruits spun in a fruity ballet,
While cherries twirled, a cabaret!

But when the pineapple tried to impress,
He tripped and bumped into the press.
With laughter that echoed through shadows so deep,
The fruits partied on, not missing a beat!

Embrace of Citrus Sunbeams

In a garden of bright zesty dreams,
Bees dance like they've joined some cool teams.
Lemons wink, as limes make a fuss,
While guavas do splits on the bus!

Sunshine tickles the tulips' toes,
As butterflies giggle in funny rows.
Radishes prank with a twist and shout,
Telling the carrots what it's all about!

The apricots wear their sombreros proud,
While the cantaloupes sway with the crowd.
Pineapples strut with flair and snaps,
Creating a party for all the chaps!

So let's sip on giggles from citrus cups,
And ride on the backs of bouncy pups.
With voices that bubble and burst with glee,
In this sun-kissed land of fruity jubilee!

Hues of a Melodic Spring

A ukulele brings a joyful jingle,
While daisies spin round, as sweet songs mingle.
The tulips steal moves from the daffodils,
In a floral dance, laughter spills!

The skies are painted with giggles and grins,
As paper airplanes start their spins.
Hummingbirds hum a tune so light,
As petals say, 'Hold on tight!'

Strawberries shrugged off their winter coats,
Singing with berries in funny floats.
While rainbow sprinkles rain down from the trees,
Turning all moments into joyous tease!

In this palette of vivid delight,
Where laughter and color take flight.
We bounce and twirl in a cheerful fling,
To this merry beat of the melodious spring!

Sweetness in the Gentle Wind

The breeze tickles grass, oh, what a tease,
As candy floss flutters on joyful knees.
Cotton candy clouds drift and flip,
While caramel puddles are begging a dip.

Fruits are chatting, as friends do align,
With tangerines giggling, sharing their wine.
Honeydew whispers sweet nothings near,
While jellies are wobbling, full of cheer!

A cupcake parade rolls down the lane,
With frosting confetti dancing like rain.
Lollipops march on sugar-coated feet,
Creating a wondrous, whimsical beat!

The wind carries laughter with zesty tunes,
Under the gaze of the chuckling moons.
Join the frolic, don't let it end,
In this whirlwind of sweetness, my friend!

Chasing the Canopy of Light

Under dappled sunlight, we skip and twirl,
Chasing shadows that swirl like a pearl.
The breeze whispers secrets of ticklish trails,
As we're pirates in pursuit of fruity tales!

Lemonade rivers flow with giggly glee,
While raspberry clouds float so carefree.
The sun winks down with a cheeky grin,
As our laughter dances gently in the din.

Marigolds gossip about our feat,
As squirrels join in, beating tiny feet.
The canopy giggles with mischiefs galore,
Inviting us in for a wild encore!

So let's ride this breeze, run 'til we tire,
In a world blooming with warmth and fire.
For in each ray of sunshine, we find our fate,
With playful hearts, let's celebrate!

Journey through Whispering Petals

In a garden filled with giggles,
Each petal sings a tune,
I tripped on my own two feet,
And danced beneath the moon.

Butterflies laugh in the aire,
Sipping nectar, quite the sight,
I think they're up to mischief,
With giggly games all night.

The bees buzz like old friends,
Sharing jokes in flowery jest,
While I try to catch my breath,
In this pollen-filled fest.

A breeze blows, tickles my nose,
As I chase a potential prank,
Fell into a rose bush,
Oh goodness, how I sank!

Awakening in Citrus's Lullaby

Snoozing under citrus trees,
Dreams go zipping by,
A squirrel steals my sandwich,
While I let out a sigh.

The lemons laugh in the sun,
With zesty jibes all day,
I joined their citrus band,
But they did not want to play.

The sweetness of the oranges,
Danced along the way,
But my shoes are too sticky,
Oh, what a sunny fray!

With a wink and a leap,
I twist, shimmy, and twirl,
Tripped over my own two feet,
And fell in to a whirl!

Sun-Eyed Daydreams

Under a sky so blue,
I try to take a nap,
But the sun's too bright and cheeky,
Slapping me with a clap.

Lemons wear sunglasses,
Tanning in the light,
While ants hold a dance-off,
On my picnic delight.

The daisies start to gossip,
About my stylish hat,
They say it looks like jellybeans,
I think I'll have a chat.

I close my eyes and giggle,
As the world spins by in shades,
I'm just a silly dreamer,
In a bowl of citrus made!

Bliss of the Warm Afternoon

The afternoon sun chuckles,
Tickling leaves up high,
I serve a cup of laughter,
To the clouds drifting by.

The warmth wraps me in a hug,
As I stroll down the lane,
But watch out for that puddle,
I leap and land on a train!

Sunflowers throw confetti,
As I waddle and bob,
If life's a big fruit salad,
I surely am the squab!

I chase a rolling orange,
With a giggle and a spin,
In this blissful warm afternoon,
I feel like I just win!

The Lightness of Sunkissed Breeze

The sun plays tag with lazy clouds,
While flowers giggle in the fields.
A bee dives in, all draped in gold,
Mistaking nectar for fine meals.

The breeze whispers secrets from afar,
Tickling leaves like a playful cat.
Dandelions dance, not caring who sees,
As squirrels wear hats, it's quite the spat.

Lemonade laughs in the summer heat,
A cheeky lime joins in the fun.
The grass winks, inviting all to meet,
Underneath the glowing afternoon sun.

So grab a snack, join the merry crew,
The joyous mayhem calls your name.
Here life is sweet, and laughter is true,
In this whimsical, sunlit game.

Serenade of Garden Delights

In the garden, where veggies jive,
A carrot twirls, a cabbage swoops.
Radishes laugh as they come alive,
While peas play poker in little groups.

Tomatoes blush, they think they're stars,
As butterflies hover with grace and charm.
The raccoon croons under moonlit bars,
Singing softly, "Don't cause any harm!"

Jasmine scents a playful breeze,
Tickling noses with floral surprise.
A sunflower giggles, "If you please,
Join the fiesta where joy never dies!"

So come and join this merry ball,
Where veggies strut and flowers sway.
In the garden, there's fun for all,
A serenade that brightens the day!

Enchanted Citrus Gardens

In a grove where sunlight beams,
Lemons laugh, and oranges grin.
A squirrel spins, lost in dreams,
While grapefruit waltzes with a dollop of gin.

Pineapples sport their spiky crowns,
As limes tell tales of zesty times.
Beneath the shade, nobody frowns,
Even the soil carries rhythm and rhymes.

Lemonade rivers and orange streams,
Flow through fields of joyous cheer.
Everything here bursts with gleams,
And even the weeds seem to disappear.

So join the dance in this wonderland,
Where everything brightens the mood.
With laughter and joy there's no command,
Just citrus fun, wildly imbued!

Breezes that Carry Sweetness

Winds arrive with a cheeky grin,
Swirling scents of sugary delight.
Cotton candy clouds gently spin,
As giggling flowers greet the light.

Butterflies float on the laughter breeze,
Stealing secrets from tulip's fold.
With candy-coated leaves and glee,
Every moment is a story told.

In the meadow where joy ignites,
Honey drips like sunshine drops.
Bees juggle blooms in playful sights,
While everyone around just hops.

So lift your spirits, let them soar,
Join the fun that nature brings.
With breezes sweet, who could ask for more?
Life's a treat where laughter sings!

Sweet Zest Upon the Breath

In the garden, bees do dance,
With a buzz and subtle prance.
Sour lemons stick to their wing,
While they sing, oh, what a fling!

Limes wear hats, and oranges boast,
Dancing fruits, we love the most.
Twirling under sunny skies,
With their laughter, we all rise!

Grapefruits giggle, round and bright,
Tickling each other with delight.
Slice a fruit and hear them scream,
It's a juicy, zesty dream!

Lemonade smiles, hugs galore,
As the fruits all start to roar.
With a wink, they take a leap,
Joyful secrets they will keep!

Horizon of Citrus Delight

A sunny day with zest to spare,
Limes are lounging, without a care.
Pomelo's playing peek-a-boo,
While tangerines form a hullabaloo!

Clouds are puffs of fluffy cream,
While fruits share their silly dream.
Uplifting tales of sweet surprise,
With all the laughs and sunny skies!

Citrus cups fill up with smiles,
As we juggle bright fruits for miles.
Sipping sunshine, oh so fine,
Each fruit a comical design!

Underneath the citrus sun,
Every moment feels like fun.
High-fives exchanged with every zest,
In this fruity, funny fest!

Flourish of Tangerine Glow

Dancing citrus, what a sight,
Twisting, turning, pure delight.
Tiny hands of tangy cheer,
Waving at all who wander near!

Chasing clouds, with zest we blend,
Mischievous fruits, they won't end.
Bananas wear their peel like capes,
As they prance in silly shapes!

Underneath the tangerine hue,
Lemon drops join in the brew.
Orange giggles float through the air,
Making all the world more rare!

With each bounce, the fruits collide,
In this punchy, zesty ride.
So let's laugh till our sides ache,
For every fruit is fun to take!

Breezy Days of Petal Whispers

Petals flutter, saying hi,
While fruits roll and laugh, oh my!
Peachy giggles fill the breeze,
Chasing with childhood tease!

Breezy days of fun galore,
Citrus antics we adore.
Wondering what else they'll do,
As they dance in brilliant hue!

Daffodils join the fruity show,
With every turn, they steal the glow.
What a mischief-loving crew,
Their silly games are never through!

So come and join this laugh parade,
With fruity friends, we'll never fade.
In every breeze, a tickle, tease,
With laughter shared among the trees!

Sun-Kissed Aromas in the Air

The sun sneezed and it tickled the bees,
They wore tiny shades with the greatest of ease.
Butterflies giggled, swirling around,
While daisies and tulips danced on the ground.

A citrusy hitchhiker hitched a ride,
On a rolling breeze, swaying with pride.
Lemons jested, their zesty replies,
While the laughter of limes filled the skies.

A garden of puns in the playful sun,
Bouncing and bobbing, oh what fun!
With every aroma, a joke on the side,
In the sweet summer air, let laughter glide.

So come chase the scents, let your worries release,
Join in the frolic, it's time for some cheese!
With giggles and glimmers, our spirits soar,
In this fragrant circus, who could ask for more?

Scented Memories of Warmth

Mango found a hat, it was way too big,
He tripped on his laughter, danced a silly jig.
With every snicker, the warmth would grow,
As friends shared tales, in the golden glow.

Watermelon wore shoes made of cream,
While pineapples plotted a fruity daydream.
The sun painted grins on each juicy face,
In a jam of delight, we all found our place.

A peach played charades, it was simply absurd,
As nectarines cheered with each silly word.
With scents swirling up like a whimsical tease,
We wrapped up our joys in a fragrant breeze.

So come gather round, let the memories flow,
In the warmth of these scents, we all let go.
With laughter as sour as old lemonade,
Twirling in sunshine, our worries do fade.

A Dance of Citrus and Sky

Citrus critters tossed their hats in the air,
A wobbly tango, a zesty affair.
Limes did the limbo, all in a row,
While lemons performed a high-flying show.

The sun set the stage with a golden hue,
As oranges rolled in with a giggly crew.
Dancing on rooftops, they twirled with flair,
Spreading bright banter, a fruity affair.

Grapefruits giggled in a wobbly whirl,
As the dusk painted skies, a fruity swirl.
With each step they took, the air filled with cheer,
In this dance of delight, come join us, my dear!

So let's all sway under the peachy light,
With dreams of great laughs, we'll twirl through the night.

Citrus companions, such laughter we bring,
In this joyful romp, how our hearts take wing!

Breezy Hues of Golden Moments

A breeze popped the bubble of a juicy joke,
While honeyed laughter began to evoke.
With every chuckle, the sweet air would twine,
Like ribbons of sunshine, oh how they'd shine!

The sassy papaya teased the ripe berry,
As the clouds floated by, all light and merry.
The sun winked down, sharing giggles and cheer,
Creating a canvas where fun sparks appear.

Mango hats flew in the sky's playful kick,
With splashes of humor painted quick!
We danced through the colors, our hearts full of glee,
In a world of bright laughter, come dance along with me!

The days may roll by, like fruit in a bowl,
But the joyous moments candy the soul.
So gather your giggles, let joy set the pace,
In this breezy saga, we all find our place!

Zestful Tides of the Heart

A frog in the sun, with a splash and a hop,
He stole my ice cream, but I just can't stop.
With citrusy grins and lemonade smiles,
We dance through the fields for a couple of miles.

The squirrels and the bees join our goofy parade,
Each step that we take feels like a charade.
The tickle of laughter, sweet as a pie,
As we chase down the clouds in a bright blue sky.

The trees giggle softly as they sway to our tune,
While we skip past the daisies that grow 'neath the moon.
A jester's delight in the breeze so sublime,
Bouncing through shadows, we're lost in our rhyme.

So here's to the moments, both silly and bright,
When laughter and joy fill our hearts with pure light.
With goofy adventures under sunshine's embrace,
Life's sweetest delights are found in each space.

Colorful Echoes in the Florals

A parrot named Bob wore a bright little hat,
He danced with a flower, and oh, how they sat!
In the garden of giggles where petals take flight,
He told the dumb joke that made the sun bright.

The tulips were snickering, the roses went red,
When Bob cracked the punchline, a funny thing spread.
With bees in a chorus, they buzzed all around,
Join in on the laughter, quite sweetly profound!

In the garden of glee, where the colors collide,
The wind plays a tune as we chuckle beside.
Each blossom is laughing, each petal's a wink,
In this funny floral world, I don't stop to think.

So grab a potted plant, let's plant us some cheer,
With vibrant hilarity, joy's always near.
As we sway with the petals, oh what a delight,
In this riot of color, we dance through the night.

Whispered Secrets of Orchard Paths

Down in the orchard, where apples all giggle,
A crabapple tree does the silliest wiggle.
A squirrel's on a mission for berries so fine,
While I seek out secrets, some labels to find.

The peaches are plump, they wear little frowns,
As I tease them for being the silliest clowns.
The whispers of lemons, they tickle my ears,
As they gossip of grapes and their sweet, juicy years.

But wait! What's this? A pear dressed like me,
With glasses and ties—all a part of the spree!
We laugh and we frolic down paths that entwine,
In this orchard of wonder, every moment's divine.

So let's keep on wandering, with glee, side by side,
Through secrets and laughter, it's a joyful ride.
With whispers of fruit and giggles galore,
Each step is a treasure, can't wait for what's more!

A Symphony of Scented Joy

In the land of the scents, where the daisies hum,
I found a small kitten who played on a drum.
With citrusy melodies filling the air,
We danced to the rhythm, without a care.

The daisies and lilacs joined in with a cheer,
As the frog strummed a banjo, oh sweet music here!
We spun 'round in circles, with laughter so bright,
As the night turned to day, and the day turned to night.

A riotous party where wildflowers sing,
With every note played, joy's the heart of the thing.
The bumblebee duo performed quite a show,
Dancing to tunes only nature could know.

So grab all your friends, let's rejoice without end,
With petals as confetti, let the laughter blend.
In this symphony fragrant, where joy's never coy,
The music of friendship is the true scented joy.

Petals Floating in the Twilight

Petals dance like tipsy sprites,
Chasing shadows, taking flights.
A bee joins in, a buzzing clown,
Wobbling round, then tumbling down.

Laughter carried on the air,
As wobbly critters all declare.
With every swirl, a joke's retold,
While petals giggle, bold and gold.

A slight breeze teases with a grin,
As nature's jesters join the spin.
Frogs croak along, a croaky tune,
While fireflies wave with bright maroon.

In this twilight party, fun does bloom,
A scent so sweet, we'd all assume.
With petals flying, laughter gleams,
In twilight's arms where joy still beams.

A Fusion of Warmth and Scent

Mixing warmth with scents so funny,
The flowers giggle, oh so sunny.
A breeze tickles, a playful tease,
As petals wiggle on the trees.

The sun grins wide, a giant's joke,
It bathes us in a citrus cloak.
Once a serious bumblebee,
Trips on sweet nectar, now carefree.

A blend of laughter, smell, and sight,
Mice in bow ties dance with delight.
Wiggly worms in tiny hats,
Join in the fun with silly spats.

The colors burst, a pie of cheer,
As awkward critters start to steer.
This fusion brings a joyful song,
Where everyone, of course, belongs.

Rays of Light on Citrus Trails

Sunbeams waltz on trails so bright,
As laughter spills, pure delight.
Each ray tickles with a wink,
While flowers blush and joints all clink.

A playful rabbit in the sun,
Hops around; this is pure fun.
Chasing shadows like it's a race,
With giggles ringing, fills the space.

Around the bends of citrus lane,
A parade of joy, not one in vain.
Squeaky voices from the trees,
As branches sway, they dance with ease.

With rays of light, the world ignites,
And even clouds join in the sights.
This cheerful trail, a sunny cheer,
Where giggles bloom throughout the year.

Breezy Whispers of Sunlit Paths

Whispers flit on sunlit ways,
As flowers boast of funny days.
The breeze, a jokester in disguise,
Delivers puns, thin as the skies.

A squirrel juggles acorns loud,
While petals twirl, in laughter, proud.
The sunshine grins, a cosmic tease,
And nature hums with playful ease.

Dancing shadows in bright parade,
Invite all critters, unafraid.
With every gust, more giggles spread,
As honey drips from gardens fed.

In this embrace, all worries cease,
With whispers soft, we find our peace.
On sunlit paths, we weave our dreams,
In every breeze, joy brightly beams.

Languid Sighs of Spring's Kiss

The flowers giggle in the light,
They dance with bees, oh what a sight!
A squirrel throws a party near,
While all the birds sing loud and clear.

The sunbeams play on shady trees,
They tickle grass with gentle tease.
A lazy river starts to laugh,
With every frog's daring half-splash!

The fragrances take on a prank,
Whispers of scents from the fragrant bank.
A robin drops its stylish hat,
And squirrels chase, oh what of that!

So here's to the laughter we create,
Where even the flowers can't help but wait.
In every bloom, a chuckle finds,
Spring's charm unfolds in funny binds.

A Canvas of Sunlit Blooms

A canvas painted with bright delight,
Where tulips giggle in morning light.
The daisies wear their polka dots,
While pansies pose in funny spots.

Bumblebees buzzing in funky styles,
They dance like they just won the miles.
While butterflies play hide and seek,
Collecting nectar like it's a streak!

The sun sets down with a bow and wink,
While petals gossip, more than you think.
A sprout trips over a clumsy root,
Calling to worms in a silly hoot!

As laughter echoes through the air,
Nature pranks with flair and care.
In every bloom, a joy to find,
A canvas where giggles unwind.

Palette of Petal Puffs

A palette spills with colors bright,
Where roses blush with sheer delight.
Tulips blush, they spin and grin,
While daisies declare, 'Let's begin!'

Puffy clouds drift without a care,
Tempting flowers with bits to share.
A beetle does a little jig,
Then tumbles down, quite like a pig!

The wind whispers secrets in the sun,
While shadows dance, oh what fun!
Each petal wears a happy face,
In this funny floral race!

So lift your spirits, let them fly,
In the fun of spring, say goodbye!
For every puff, there's laughter drawn,
In the silly hues of the giggly dawn.

Glow of the Gentle Horizon

The horizon glows with a playful tease,
Where laughing flowers sway in the breeze.
A sunflower juggles its big yellow head,
While poppies nap, as if they're dead!

The sky is painted, oh, what a sight!
A watercolor dream in the fading light.
Where bees chase butterflies in the air,
And clouds play tag, without a care!

The gentle breeze sneaks in to play,
Tickling petals in a sneaky way.
A ladybug slips on dewy grass,
As flowers whisper, 'Oh, let it pass!'

So here's to the glow that makes us grin,
Where nature holds a carnival within.
In every hue, a chuckle lies,
In the fold of the gentle skies!

The Embrace of Springtime Air

A breeze tickles my nose, oh what a tease,
It wiggles and jigs, plays games with the trees.
The flowers start laughing, they nod and they sway,
While I sneeze in surprise, thinking spring's here to stay.

A butterfly flops, oh dear, is that a dance?
I feel quite important, given the chance.
With petals all buzzing and bees on parade,
I'm suddenly dizzy, should have worn a spade!

The sun throws confetti, a bright golden stream,
While squirrels look on as if caught in a dream.
A duck quacks her laughter, a jester so bold,
In this raucous delight, I forget I am old.

As I twirl to the rhythm of life's playful tune,
I trip over daisies beneath the sweet moon.
With laughter like bubbles, I float through the air,
Letting spring's silly vibe entwine in my hair.

Beneath the Golden Canopy

Underneath branches dressed bright golden cheer,
The humor's contagious, it's laughter I hear.
A squirrel takes stage, with nuts as his bling,
He juggles his treasures, oh what a fun thing!

The daisies are grinning, the roses play coy,
While I, in the middle, just giggle with joy.
A breeze steals my hat, and it's off on a run,
I chase it through gardens, oh what silly fun!

The sun's crayons splash colors on everything near,
While worms do a tango, all wiggly cheer.
The daisies all shout, "You can dance with us too!"
As petals rain down, like confetti on cue.

With giggles abounding, I bow to the scene,
In laughter and whispers, we share in the green.
The sun dips its head, but it's still quite the show,
Beneath the grand canopy, happiness flows.

Dancing Through Flowered Avenues

On pathways of petals, I prance to the beat,
With blooms all around, oh what a sweet treat!
A ladybug twirls, in a polka-dot gown,
She winks as she spins, not a care in this town.

The tulips are giggling, it's quite the parade,
As I sashay past, with my very own charade.
The wind starts to chortle, and I join the fun,
Each flower erupts into laughter - we run!

A bumblebee buzzes, a conductor of sorts,
As I shimmy with petals, by jolly cohorts.
With every soft step, they tickle my toes,
In this dance of the blossoms, everybody knows.

With sandals that squeak, oh what a fine jam,
I twirl as I wander, I'm enjoying the slam.
The day fades to dusk, yet still, here I prance,
In this waltz of the flowers, I happily dance.

Floral Secrets of the Sunset

The sun whispers secrets, so sweet and so bright,
While flowers confide under softening light.
With giggles and winks, they share their sweet lore,
As shadows grow long, and the fireflies soar.

A cactus with charm gives a sassy salute,
"Don't take life too seriously! Dance in your boots!"
The daisies nod softly, and the lilies chime in,
As the day's laughter tumbles, where does it begin?

The tulips swap tales of mischief and glee,
While daisies tell stories of how to be free.
In the twilight's embrace, all the night blooms conspire,
To fill up the world with their glowing desire.

So, let's gather giggles and sprinkle them wide,
Around every corner, let's spread simple pride.
As daylight takes bow, in a gown made of blush,
Floral secrets reveal, in the breath of the hush.

Sun-Soaked Fragrance in Flight

A lazy bee has lost its map,
Now buzzing 'round like it's in a trap.
Chasing scents on sunny days,
In floral fields, it finds new ways.

With pollen stuck to every wing,
It looks just like a fluffy king.
It's confused, but what a sight,
Bumping flowers in sheer delight.

Bees might dance and frolic gay,
But surely lose the game of tag play.
They twirl in circles, oh what clowns,
As petals scatter, joy abounds!

So when you see that buzzing show,
Remember they're just putting on a glow.
In sunshine's warmth, they frolic free,
In their sweet world, a comedy!

Breeze-Kissed Petal Dreams

The wind whispers with a cheeky grin,
Tickling petals and making them spin.
A great big flower starts to sway,
Excited by a breezy play.

A lilac laughs, a daisy sneezes,
While roses blush, losing their breezes.
Then comes a gust, a floral ballet,
Leaves and petals all dance away!

Bees giggle in sunshine's flair,
As dandelions spread without a care.
They tumble and roll, what a sight!
Chasing dreams in the soft sunlight.

Fluttering about like a happy sprite,
Petals tumble, a cheerful flight.
In breezes so merry, flowers bloom,
Creating a carnival in full zoom!

Sunlit Whispers of Flora

The garden's alive with giggles and sighs,
As daisies tell secrets beneath the blue skies.
In sun-kissed patches, they share their tales,
Of runaway bees and wobbling snails.

Lavender says, 'I smell quite divine!'
While the tulips roll, declaring, 'I shine!'
What a ruckus, a floral choir,
With laughter that thrums, lifting them higher.

In the shadows, shy violets peek,
Eavesdropping on gossip, so sweet and chic.
"Oh dear, did you hear? What a blunder!"
While sunbeams tickle, making them wonder.

Each petal vibrates with joy and cheer,
Creating a riddle that all can hear.
In this sunlit garden, there's never a gloom,
Where flowers and laughter forever bloom!

The Allure of Floral Whirls

In a whirlwind of colors, flowers collide,
Dancing around, they toss aside pride.
Pansies giggle, and tulips prance,
In this wacky, flowery dance.

A rogue breeze comes, making them spin,
Petals scatter, laughter within.
"Oh, catch me!" whispers a shy bloom,
Swirling and twirling, filling the room!

Carnations joke, "I'm building a wall!"
As garden gnomes smile, watching it all.
A sight so funny, all hues in a flurry,
In a world where nature has no worry.

With every swerve and silly flight,
Flowers perform in pure sunlight.
The petals laugh, the colors whirl,
In this glorious and vibrant swirl!

Whirling in Sunlit Essence

In the garden, dancing bees,
With tiny hats and tiny knees.
They sip from cups that never spill,
Buzzing laughter, what a thrill!

Sunbeams bounce, like kids at play,
Chasing shadows throughout the day.
The daisies giggle, the roses tease,
Nature's jesters, oh such ease!

A daffodil dons a jaunty bow,
While tulips sway, take a bow somehow.
The air is filled with silly tunes,
As squirrels join in, under the moons.

Laughter swells with every gust,
In this realm of bloom and rust.
Joyful pranks in colorful fields,
Sharing secrets that nature yields.

Aromas of Early Spring

A whiff of mischief in the breeze,
As sneaky snails crawl with such ease.
Each petal whispers a laughing tune,
Underneath the giggling moon.

The tulips prance with flair and style,
They wink at clouds, go on, beguile!
The daisies play a game of hide,
Poking fun from every side.

When the breeze blows a ticklish song,
Butterflies dance, where they belong.
They toss their wings in a playful spin,
Creating chaos—the laughter begins!

The sun beams down with a cheeky grin,
As if it knows that it's set to win.
In this merry patch of vibrant cheer,
Every fragrance adds to the fun near.

Cascades of Blushing Blooms

Flower capers, they're on display,
With petals winking, come join the fray.
The sun's a jester, bright and bold,
Spreading laughter, worth its weight in gold.

Beneath the azure, daisies frolic,
Embracing all in a dance, symbolic.
Poppy pods share jokes that confound,
While butterflies spin round and round.

Each blossom has a tale to tell,
Of prankster ants and smirking bell.
A chorus of colors, they take flight,
Creating whimsy—what a sight!

The fragrance giggles, soft and bright,
As blooms unite in sheer delight.
A merry chase, where mischief looms,
In cascading waves of vibrant blooms.

Petal-Powered Journeys

On petal boats, they sail away,
With laughter guiding their merry play.
The bees are captains, which is grand,
Navigating through a flowered land.

A rogue wind comes and spins them 'round,
Making tumbling tales abound.
Laughing stems sway from side to side,
In this joyful, wild petal ride.

Pollen dust on their tiny feet,
Turning every step into a treat.
They sing of joys both big and small,
In this fun-filled, flowery ball.

So come aboard this fragrant train,
Where each bloom smiles, never in vain.
The journey's laughter, sweet and clear,
In every petal, joy draws near.

www.ingramcontent.com/pod-product-compliance
Lightning Source LLC
Chambersburg PA
CBHW060146230426
43661CB00003B/592